A Nest Is

By Liza Charlesworth

ISBN: 978-1-339-02686-2

Art Director: Tannaz Fassihi; Designer: Tanya Chernyak
Photos © Getty Images and Shutterstock.com.
Copyright © Liza Charlesworth. All rights reserved. Published by Scholastic Inc.

3 4 5 6 7 8 9 10   68   32 31 30 29 28 27 26 25 24

Printed in Jiaxing, China. First printing, August 2023.

See the snug nest.
It has chicks in it!
A nest is a home.

A nest can be made of twigs.
It can be made of mud
or bits of grass.

A nest is a spot to rest.
It's a spot to get a snack
from mom. Gulp!

See the nest up in the tree.
It's a home for lots of bugs.
Buzz, buzz, buzz!

See the nest at the pond.
It's a home for ducks.
They can hop in and swim.

This nest is in the sand.
It has eggs in it.
They are croc eggs!

Crack, crack!
Croc tots pop from the eggs.
A nest is a snug home!